WHAT IS THE BOOK OF DEUTERONOMY?

Kids' Guides to God's Word Series

What Is the Book of Genesis?
What Is the Book of Exodus?
What Is the Book of Leviticus?
What Is the Book of Numbers?
What Is the Book of Deuteronomy?
What Is the Book of Joshua?
What Is the Book of Judges?
What Is the Book of Ruth?
What Is the Book of 1 Samuel?
What Is the Book of 2 Samuel?
What Is the Book of 1 Kings?
What Is the Book of 2 Kings?
What Are the Books of 1–2 Chronicles?
What Are the Books of Ezra & Nehemiah?
What Is the Book of Esther?
What Is the Book of Job?
What Is the Book of Psalms?
What Is the Book of Proverbs?
What Is the Book of Ecclesiastes?
What Are the Books of Song of Songs &
Lamentations?
What Is the Book of Isaiah?
What Is the Book of Jeremiah?
What Is the Book of Ezekiel?
What Is the Book of Daniel?
What Are the Books of Hosea–Micah?
What Are the Books of Nahum–Malachi?

What Is the Gospel of Matthew?
What Is the Gospel of Mark?
What Is the Gospel of Luke?
What Is the Gospel of John?
What Is the Book of Acts?
What Is the Book of Romans?
What Is the Book of 1 Corinthians?
What Is the Book of 2 Corinthians?
What Is the Book of Galatians?
What Is the Book of Ephesians?
What Is the Book of Philippians?
What Are the Books of Colossians
& Philemon?
What Are the Books of 1–2 Thessalonians?
What Are the Books of 1–2 Timothy & Titus?
What Is the Book of Hebrews?
What Is the Book of James?
What Are the Books of 1–2 Peter & Jude?
What Are the Books of 1–3 John?
What Is the Book of Revelation?

What Is the Book of
DEUTERONOMY?

Michael Whitworth

ISBN 978-1-971767-08-6

Published by Start2Finish
Bend, Oregon 97702
start2finish.org

Printed in the United States of America
30 29 28 27 26   1 2 3 4 5

CONTENTS

INTRODUCTION

Have you ever had to say goodbye to someone who mattered more to you than you could put into words? Maybe it was a grandparent who sat you down and told you things they wanted you to remember, things about your family, about life, about what really matters when everything else falls away. Maybe it was a coach or a teacher who pulled you aside on the last day of school and said something you've never forgotten. Maybe it was a friend who was moving away, and you both knew that whatever you said in those final minutes would have to last a long time.

There's a weight to last words. People don't waste them. When someone knows they're running out of time, they don't talk about the weather. They talk about the things that matter most. They say what they've been meaning to say. They hold nothing back.

That's the book of Deuteronomy. It's the last words of the most important leader Israel ever had, spoken to the people he loved, on the last day of his life.

WHERE WE ARE IN THE STORY

To understand Deuteronomy, you need to know what came before it. In Genesis, God made a promise to a man named Abraham: his descendants would become a great nation, inherit a land of their own, and bless the entire world. Abraham believed the promise, but he never saw it fulfilled. Neither did his son or his grandson.

In Exodus, Abraham's descendants had grown into the nation of Israel, but they were slaves in Egypt. God raised up Moses, sent ten devastating plagues, and led his people out through the Red Sea. He brought them to Mount Sinai, gave them the Ten Commandments, and made a covenant with them. Then he told them to build a tabernacle, a tent where his presence would dwell right in the middle of their camp.

In Leviticus, God explained how a sinful people could live in the presence of a holy God. Every sacrifice, every ritual, every law existed to answer one question: how can God dwell among us without destroying us?

In Numbers, everything fell apart. Israel reached the border of the Promised Land but refused to enter because they were afraid of the people living there. God's response was devastating: that entire generation would die in the wilderness. For forty years, Israel wandered in circles while a generation of rebels grew old and died. Only their children would inherit the promise.

Now comes Deuteronomy. The forty years are over. The old generation is gone. A new generation stands on the plains of Moab, east of the Jordan River, close enough to see the land God promised Abraham five hundred years earlier. The tabernacle is behind them. The Jordan is in front of them. And Moses, the man who led them out of Egypt, through the sea, and across the desert, is about to die.

He knows it. God has told him. Because of his own failure to honor God at a critical moment, Moses will not be crossing the Jordan with his people. He will see the Promised Land from a mountaintop, but he will never set foot in it.

So Moses does the only thing he can do. He gathers the entire nation, every man, woman, child, and foreigner among them, and he preaches. He preaches like a man who knows these are the last words anyone will ever hear from him. He retells their story. He restates the law. He warns them, pleads with them, challenges them, and pours out everything he has into one final, passionate appeal.

Deuteronomy is that appeal.

WHAT YOU'RE ABOUT TO READ

The name "Deuteronomy" comes from a Greek word meaning "second law." But that's a little misleading. This isn't a second set of rules. It's a second telling of the same law, repreached by Moses to a generation that needs to hear it for themselves. Think of it less as a legal document and more as a farewell sermon from a preacher who has been ministering to this congregation for four decades.

The book breaks into three major speeches, followed by a series of closing events.

Moses' first speech (chapters 1–4) looks backward. He retells the story of Israel's journey from Sinai to Moab, reminding the new generation of their parents' failures and of God's faithfulness despite those failures. He warns them not to forget what God has done and not to repeat the mistakes of the past.

Moses' second speech (chapters 5–28) is the longest and most important section. It restates the Ten Commandments, introduces the most famous prayer in Jewish history—"Hear, O Israel: The Lord our God, the Lord is one. Love the Lord your God with all your heart and with all your soul and with all your strength"—and then works out what loyalty to God looks like in every corner of life: worship, justice, leadership, family, business, war, and care for the poor. It ends with the blessings that will follow obedience and the curses that will follow rebellion, laid out in devastating detail.

Moses' third speech (chapters 29–30) is the emotional climax of the book. Moses renews the covenant with this generation and delivers some of the most powerful words in all of Scripture: "I have set before you life and death, blessings and curses. Now choose life."

The final chapters (31–34) record Moses' last actions: commissioning Joshua as his successor, writing down the law, teaching the people a song to remember, blessing the twelve tribes, and climbing Mount Nebo to see the land he will never enter. Then Moses dies. And God buries him in a grave no one has ever found.

WHY THIS BOOK MATTERS

You might be thinking: a book of sermons from three thousand years ago? Why should I care?

Because Jesus quoted Deuteronomy more often than any other book in the Old Testament. When Satan tempted Jesus in the wilderness, every single answer Jesus gave came from Deuteronomy. When someone asked Jesus which commandment was the greatest, he quoted Deuteronomy. This book mattered to Jesus more than almost any other. If it shaped the way he understood God, resisted temptation, and defined his mission, it's worth your attention too.

But Deuteronomy also matters because it speaks directly to a problem every generation faces: the danger of forgetting. Moses knew that the generation standing before him was passionate today but might be indifferent tomorrow. He knew that prosperity has a way of making people forget where they came from. He knew that the children of believers don't automatically believe. Faith has to be taught. It has to be passed on. It has to be chosen.

That's why Moses keeps saying "remember" and "don't forget." That's why he tells parents to talk about God's commands when they sit at home and walk along the road, when they lie down and when they get up. That's why he writes the law on stones, teaches the people a song, and commissions Joshua in front of the whole nation. He's doing everything in his power to make sure the truth outlasts him.

And underneath it all, Deuteronomy is about something beautifully simple: God wants to be with his people. The covenant, the laws, the warnings, the blessings, the curses, all of it exists because the God of the universe looked at a nation of former slaves and said, "You are mine. I love you. Stay close."

BEFORE YOU BEGIN

Deuteronomy is not a difficult book to read, but it does have some features worth knowing about.

There's repetition. Moses says the same things more than once, sometimes in nearly the same words. That's not sloppy writing. It's preaching. When something matters enough, you say it again. And again.

There's hard content. The blessings and curses of chapter 28 are among the most intense passages in the Bible. The command to drive out the Canaanites raises real questions. We'll address these honestly as they come.

And there's a death at the end that will hit harder than you expect. Moses has been the voice of these first five books of the Bible since Exodus 2. When he climbs that mountain for the last time, you'll feel it.

But most of all, there's grace. Deuteronomy is sometimes dismissed as a book of law, but from beginning to end it's a book about a God who rescues people who don't deserve it, stays with people who keep wandering away, and offers life to people who keep choosing death.

That's the God Moses wants you to meet.

So here we are, standing on the plains of Moab with two million Israelites and one old prophet who's running out of time. The Jordan is ahead. The land is waiting. And Moses has a few things left to say. Let's listen.

Turn the page.

1

REMEMBER THE ROAD

Jules Verne wrote a novel in 1872 about a wealthy Englishman named Phileas Fogg who makes a wild bet: he can travel around the entire world in eighty days. The whole book is a race against time. Fogg and his servant Passepartout hop from steamships to trains to elephants to wind-powered sleds, running into disaster after disaster, missing connections, getting arrested, losing days they can't afford to lose. At every turn, it looks like they won't make it. And what makes the story so gripping is how tight the schedule is. Eighty days to circle the globe. Not a day to waste.

Now imagine the opposite problem. Imagine a journey that should have taken *eleven days* but somehow stretched into *forty years*. Not because the terrain was impossible. Not because there were no roads. But because the people making the trip refused to trust the God who was leading them.

That's the story Moses tells in the opening chapters of Deuteronomy. And he's not telling it for the first time. He's telling it *again*, to a generation that needs to hear it before they make the same mistakes.

MOSES' FAREWELL

Deuteronomy opens on the edge of the Promised Land. The Israelites are camped on the plains of Moab, east of the Jordan River, so close to Canaan they could practically see the vineyards. Forty years have passed since God brought them out of Egypt. The tabernacle has traveled with them every step of the way. The pillar of cloud and fire has guided them through the wilderness. And now, finally, a new generation stands where their parents once stood, facing the same choice their parents faced.

But there's a problem. Most of this generation was too young to remember the big events. They didn't see the Red Sea part. They don't remember the thunder at Sinai. They were toddlers, or not yet born, when their parents made the decision that changed everything. They've grown up in the desert, eating manna and following a cloud, but they may not fully understand *why* they've been out here so long or *what went wrong* the first time.

Moses knows he's about to die. God has already told him he won't be crossing the Jordan. So before he leaves the stage, he does what any good preacher or teacher would do: he gathers the people and tells them the story. Their story. From the beginning.

That's what Deuteronomy is. The name means "second law," but it's not really a second set of rules. It's Moses' farewell sermon, his final set of speeches to the people he's led for four decades. He's not just repeating old information. He's preaching. He's pleading. He's begging this new generation to learn from the past and choose a different path.

And it all starts with a history lesson.

THE ELEVEN-DAY JOURNEY

Moses begins by taking the people back to Mount Sinai, which Deuteronomy calls Horeb. That's where God first spoke to Israel, gave them the Ten Commandments, and made a covenant with them. After about a year camped at that mountain, God told them it was time to move. "You have stayed long enough at this mountain," he said. "Turn and take your journey. Go to the hill country of the Amorites and take possession of the land I swore to give your fathers."

The journey from Horeb to the southern border of Canaan, a place called Kadesh Barnea, was about eleven days on foot. Eleven days. That's it. God had already promised them the land. He had already shown them his power in Egypt. All they had to do was trust him, march forward, and take what he was giving them.

They didn't.

Moses reminds the people of what happened next. When they reached Kadesh Barnea, they sent twelve spies into the land to check it out. The spies came back with an encouraging report about the land itself: it was good, fertile, everything God had promised. But ten of the twelve spies were terrified by the people living there. "They're stronger than us," they said. "The cities are huge and fortified. We even saw giants."

And that was enough. The Israelites panicked. They didn't just get nervous; they turned on God. They grumbled in their tents and said something stunning: "It is because the Lord *hates* us that he brought us out of Egypt, to hand us over to the Amorites to be destroyed."

Think about that for a second. The God who sent plagues to free them, who parted the sea to save them, who fed them bread from heaven and carried them through the desert like a father carries his child on his back, and they accused him of *hating* them. All because the obstacles in front of them looked bigger than the God behind them.

Moses tried to talk them down. "Don't be terrified," he said. "The Lord your God, who goes before you, will fight for you, just as he did in Egypt, before your very eyes." He reminded them of everything they'd seen. The fire. The cloud. The daily provision. God had never failed them. Not once.

It didn't matter. They refused to go.

TOO LATE

God's response was devastating. He swore an oath: not a single person from that faithless generation would see the Promised Land. The adults who had witnessed the miracles in Egypt but still refused to trust him would die in the wilderness. Only their children, the ones who were too young to be held responsible, would eventually inherit the land. And only two men from that generation would survive: Caleb and Joshua, the two spies who had trusted God when everyone else gave in to fear.

Then came a tragic twist. After hearing God's judgment, the people suddenly changed their minds. "We have sinned," they said. "We'll go up and fight now." But it was too late. God told them not to go, because he would not be with them. They went anyway, charging up the hill in their own strength, and the Amorites chased them back like a swarm of bees. They came home defeated, and they wept before God. But he didn't listen.

And so the long, slow dying began. For thirty-eight years, Israel wandered in circles through the wilderness. An entire generation grew old and died without ever reaching the land God had promised them. An eleven-day journey became a forty-year funeral march. Not because the distance was too great, but because their faith was too small.

VICTORIES AND HEARTBREAK

Moses doesn't stop with the failure at Kadesh Barnea. He walks the new generation through the rest of the journey: the years of wandering, the nations they passed through without fighting because God had given those lands to other peoples, and then the turning point, when God finally told them it was time to move again.

He tells them about the victories over two powerful kings east of the Jordan: Sihon, king of the Amorites, and Og, king of Bashan. Og was a giant of a man, the last of an ancient race of warriors, and even he fell before Israel because God was fighting for them. These victories mattered. They were proof, right there in living memory, that when Israel trusted God, he delivered. The land east of the Jordan was divided among the tribes of Reuben, Gad, and the half-tribe of Manasseh, with the understanding that their fighting men would still help the rest of the nation conquer the land to the west.

Then Moses shares something deeply personal. He tells the people that he begged God to let him cross the Jordan. "O Sovereign Lord," he prayed, "let me go over and see the good land beyond the Jordan, that fine hill country." It's a heartbreaking moment. Moses had given his entire life to leading these people toward a destination he would never reach. But God said no. He told Moses to stop asking. He could climb a mountain and *see* the land, but he would never set foot in it.

Instead, God told Moses to encourage Joshua, who would lead the people across. Even in his own disappointment, Moses had to prepare someone else to finish what he started.

NO GOD LIKE OURS

By chapter 4, Moses shifts from telling the story to applying it. His tone changes. He's not just a historian anymore; he's a preacher, and his sermon is urgent.

"Hear now, O Israel," he says. "Follow the decrees and laws I am about to teach you, so that you may live and go in and take possession of the land."

His argument is simple but powerful. He points to the nations around them and asks a rhetorical question: "What other nation is so great as to have their gods near them the way the Lord our God is near us whenever we pray to him? And what other nation is so great as to have such righteous decrees and laws?"

No other nation. No other god. Israel's God wasn't a distant force or a silent statue. He spoke. He listened. He was *near*. And the laws he gave weren't burdens designed to crush them. They were instructions for how to live well, how to be free, how to build a society so just and wise that other nations would look at Israel and say, "Surely this is a wise and understanding people."

But Moses also warns them. He tells them not to forget what they've seen. He tells them to teach these things to their children and their grandchildren, so the story doesn't die. He warns them specifically against idolatry, against making images or worshiping the sun, moon, and stars, because those things were created objects, not the Creator. The God who spoke from the fire at Sinai has no shape or form. He cannot be reduced to wood and stone.

And then Moses looks into the future and sees trouble coming. He tells them plainly: if they forget the covenant and turn to idols, God will scatter them among the nations. They'll end up serving gods of wood and stone that can't see, hear, eat, or smell. The irony is brutal. You want to worship lifeless things? Fine. But you'll do it in exile, far from the land I'm giving you.

But even here, Moses doesn't end without hope. "When you are in distress and all these things have happened to you," he says, "then you will return to the Lord your God and obey him. For the Lord your God is a merciful God; he will not abandon you or destroy you or forget the covenant with your ancestors."

That's the God Moses wants this generation to know. A God who disciplines but doesn't destroy. A God who judges but never forgets his promises. A God whose mercy runs deeper than his people's failures.

WHAT THIS MEANS FOR US

First, the past is never just the past. Moses didn't tell Israel's story because it was interesting. He told it because a generation that forgets where it came from is a generation that's about to repeat the same mistakes. We need to know our own stories, the stories of God's faithfulness in our families, in our churches, in our lives, because those memories are the fuel for future faith.

Second, fear is not the same as wisdom. The Israelites at Kadesh Barnea weren't being cautious. They were being faithless. There's a difference between wisely counting the cost and refusing to trust God because the obstacles look too big. Fear told them the giants were too strong. Faith would have reminded them that their God was stronger.

Third, delayed obedience is still disobedience. When Israel tried to enter the land *after* God told them not to, it wasn't faith. It was presumption. They wanted the result without the relationship. Obedience means doing what God says, when he says it, not when it finally feels convenient.

Fourth, God's "no" is not the end of the story. Moses was denied his deepest wish, and it must have crushed him. But God's refusal didn't mean God had abandoned him. Sometimes God says no to what we want because he's working on something bigger than our personal plans. Moses never entered the land, but his faithfulness shaped the people who did.

Fifth, there is no god like ours. Moses' argument in chapter 4 is as relevant today as it was three thousand years ago. The God of the Bible isn't distant or silent. He speaks. He listens. He draws near. He gives instructions that lead to life. And when his people wander away, he leaves the door open for them to come back.

TALKING POINTS

1. **Moses compared God to a father who carries his child through danger.** How does that image shape the way you think about God? Have you ever felt "carried" by God through a hard time?

2. **The Israelites saw incredible miracles but still refused to trust God when things got scary.** Why do you think it's so easy to forget what God has done when a new challenge comes along?

3. **Moses told the people not to add to or take away from God's commands.** Why do you think that warning was so important? What does it look like when people try to change what God has said to make it easier or more comfortable?

4. **God told Moses "no" when he asked to enter the Promised Land.** How do you handle it when God doesn't give you what you desperately want? What can Moses' response teach us about dealing with disappointment?

5. **Moses said that Israel's laws were supposed to make other nations admire their wisdom.** What does it look like today for God's people to live in a way that makes others take notice?

Moses has told the people where they've been. He's reminded them what went wrong. He's warned them about what could go wrong again. And he's pointed them to a God whose mercy outlasts every failure.

But he's not done. The history lesson was only the beginning. Now it's time for the heart of the covenant, the words that would define Israel's relationship with God more than any other.

Turn the page.

2

THE HEART OF EVERYTHING

Charles Dickens wrote a story about a man who gave his whole heart to the wrong thing. Ebenezer Scrooge, the miserable old miser in *A Christmas Carol*, has devoted every ounce of his energy to making money. He works obsessively. He hoards relentlessly. He squeezes every penny out of everyone around him. And it has cost him everything that actually matters. He has no friends. His family avoids him. His employee shivers in a freezing office because Scrooge won't pay for coal. The love of his life walked away years ago because she could see that money had replaced her in his heart.

Scrooge isn't broke. He's rich. But he's given his whole heart to something that can't love him back, and the result is a life that's empty, cold, and alone.

It takes three ghosts and a terrifying glimpse of his own grave to shake Scrooge awake. And when he finally wakes up on Christmas morning, transformed, the first thing he does is give. He sends a turkey to his employee's family. He donates to charity. He shows up at his nephew's house for dinner. He becomes, as Dickens puts it, "as good a friend, as good a master, and as good a man, as the good old city knew."

What changed? Not his bank account. His heart. For the first time in decades, Scrooge gave his heart to the right things: people, generosity, love. And everything else followed.

I think about Scrooge whenever I read Deuteronomy 5–6. Because these two chapters are about the same question that haunts his story: *What are you going to give your heart to?*

And the answer Moses gives is the most important sentence in the entire Old Testament.

A COVENANT FOR THIS GENERATION

After spending all of chapter 4 warning Israel about the dangers of forgetting God, Moses does something the new generation desperately needs. He takes them back to the moment that defined their nation: the day God spoke from the fire at Mount Sinai and gave them the Ten Commandments.

Most of the people standing before Moses had been children, or not yet born, when it happened. They'd heard the stories, but they hadn't stood at the base of that shaking mountain. They hadn't heard the thunder of God's voice. They hadn't felt the ground tremble under their feet. Moses knew that if these commandments were going to mean anything to this generation, they had to hear them again, not as dusty history but as a living covenant that God was making with *them*.

That's why he says something surprising at the start of chapter 5: "The Lord our God made a covenant with us at Horeb. It was not with our fathers that the Lord made this covenant, but with us, with all of us who are alive here today."

Wait. Their fathers *were* at Horeb. That's where the covenant was originally made. So what does Moses mean?

He means that a covenant with God isn't something that happened once to someone else a long time ago. It's something that every generation has to own for themselves. The previous generation had been at Sinai, yes, but they had also broken the covenant through their faithlessness and died in the wilderness. Now this generation has to step into the covenant as if it were being offered for the first time. Because in a real sense, it is.

GRACE BEFORE RULES

Then Moses restates the Ten Commandments. If you've read through Exodus, you've seen these before. But Deuteronomy's version isn't just a copy. Moses is preaching, not reciting from a legal document. He adjusts a few things, adds some explanation, and makes the commandments feel urgent and personal.

The commandments open not with a rule but with a reminder: "I am the Lord your God, who brought you out of Egypt, out of the land of slavery." That sentence matters more than most people realize. God doesn't start with "Do this" or "Don't do that." He starts with "Here's what I've already done for you." The commandments aren't the price of admission into a relationship with God. They're the response to a rescue that already happened. Grace comes first. The rules follow.

Think of it this way. The Israelites didn't earn their freedom by being good. They were slaves. They couldn't do anything to free themselves. God rescued them because he loved them and because he had made a promise to Abraham centuries earlier.

The commandments came *after* the rescue, as instructions for how a free people should live.

That's an important distinction. The commandments weren't chains. They were the opposite. They were a set of guidelines for staying free. Every single one of them protected something precious: God's honor, the family, human life, marriage, property, truth, and even the inner world of desires and contentment.

Moses walks through all ten: no other gods, no idols, don't misuse God's name, keep the Sabbath, honor your parents, don't murder, don't commit adultery, don't steal, don't lie, don't covet. In the Deuteronomy version, the Sabbath commandment gets special attention. While the Exodus version grounds it in creation (God rested on the seventh day), Moses ties it to the exodus. "Remember that you were slaves in Egypt," he says. In Egypt, they never got a day off. The Sabbath was God's gift to a people who had been worked to the bone: you are not slaves anymore, and neither is anyone in your household. Everyone rests. Everyone breathes.

After the commandments, Moses reminds the people what happened next at Sinai. The people were terrified. They had heard God's voice booming out of the fire and darkness, and they were convinced that if they heard any more, they would die. So they begged Moses to go up the mountain and listen on their behalf. "You go near and hear all that the Lord our God says," they told him. "Then tell us everything, and we will listen and obey."

God agreed. And from that point on, Moses served as the go-between, receiving God's words and passing them on to the people. That's what he's doing right now on the plains of Moab:

delivering the same message God gave him, teaching this new generation what it means to belong to God.

THE MOST IMPORTANT WORDS

And then Moses says the words. "Hear, O Israel: The Lord our God, the Lord is one. Love the Lord your God with all your heart and with all your soul and with all your strength."

This passage became the most important prayer in all of Jewish faith. For thousands of years, faithful Jews have recited it every morning and every evening. It's the first prayer Jewish children learn. It's the last words many Jews speak before they die. It was the passage Jesus quoted when someone asked him which commandment was the greatest.

So what does it mean?

The first part is a declaration: "The Lord our God, the Lord is one." This isn't a math lesson. Moses isn't saying, "God is the number one." He's saying that Israel's God is the *only* God who matters. There is no other. He's not one god among many options in a buffet line of religions. He is the God who speaks, who acts, who rescues, who keeps promises. No other so-called god has done what he has done. No other god is worthy of Israel's allegiance.

The second part is the response: "Love the Lord your God with all your heart and with all your soul and with all your strength." Every word in that sentence is doing heavy lifting.

"Heart" in the ancient world didn't just mean feelings. It meant the center of your thinking, your will, your decisions. Loving God with all your heart means giving him your mind, your choices, your plans.

"Soul" meant your whole self, your life, everything that makes you *you*. Loving God with your soul means holding nothing back.

"Strength" is the broadest word of all. Some scholars think it means something like "your everything," including your resources, your energy, your time, your possessions. Loving God with all your strength means that your devotion doesn't stop at the church door. It extends to your wallet, your schedule, your Monday morning.

Put it all together and the command is breathtaking in its scope: love God with your inner world, your whole self, and everything you have. Don't hold anything back. Don't split your loyalty. Don't give God your Sundays and someone else your heart.

This is the opposite of Scrooge. Scrooge gave his whole heart to gold. Moses says to give your whole heart to God.

THE DANGER OF FULL BELLIES

But Moses knows that saying "love God with everything" is one thing. Living it is another. So he immediately gets practical. "These commandments that I give you today are to be on your hearts. Impress them on your children. Talk about them when you sit at home and when you walk along the road, when you lie down and when you get up. Tie them as symbols on your hands and bind them on your foreheads. Write them on the doorframes of your houses and on your gates."

In other words: this isn't a Sunday-only faith. It's a breakfast-table faith. A walking-to-school faith. A last-thing-at-night and first-thing-in-the-morning faith. Moses envisions a community so saturated with the words of God that children grow up hearing them in every conversation, seeing them on every doorpost, absorbing them like the air they breathe.

The family is the classroom. The parents are the teachers. And the subject is God.

Then comes the warning. Moses knows human nature. He knows what prosperity does to people. So he describes the future in vivid terms: God is going to bring them into a land full of great cities they didn't build, houses already stocked with good things, wells already dug, vineyards already planted. They're going to eat until they're full.

"Be careful," Moses says, "that you do not forget the Lord, who brought you out of Egypt, out of the land of slavery."

When life is hard, people tend to cry out to God. When life is easy, they tend to forget him. Moses has watched this pattern his entire career. He saw it happen in the wilderness, and he knows it will happen again in Canaan. Prosperity is one of the most dangerous tests of faith there is, not because good things are bad, but because full bellies have short memories.

He also warns them not to test God, reminding them of a place called Massah, where their parents had demanded that God prove himself by providing water on their terms. Instead of trusting God to provide, they put him on trial: "Is the Lord among us or not?" It was the wrong question, asked in the wrong spirit. Moses says, Don't do that again.

TELL THE STORY

The chapter closes with one of the most beautiful passages in Deuteronomy. Moses imagines a future scene: a child asking a parent, "What is the meaning of all these laws that God commanded?"

And Moses tells the parents exactly what to say. Don't start with the rules. Start with the story.

"We were slaves of Pharaoh in Egypt, but the Lord brought us out of Egypt with a mighty hand. Before our eyes, the Lord sent signs and wonders, great and terrible, against Egypt and Pharaoh and his whole household. But he brought us out from there to bring us in, and to give us the land he promised on oath to our ancestors. The Lord commanded us to obey all these decrees and to fear the Lord our God, so that we might always prosper and be kept alive."

Did you catch the order? The story of rescue comes first. The laws come second. The meaning of the commandments is found in the story of redemption. You can't understand why God gives rules until you understand what God has done. The commands make sense only in the context of the relationship.

This is the pattern of the whole Bible. God saves, and then he shows his people how to live. He doesn't hand out instructions to strangers. He rescues people and *then* says, "Now, here's how we live together."

WHAT THIS MEANS FOR US

First, grace always comes before rules. The Ten Commandments don't start with a demand. They start with a rescue: "I am the Lord your God, who brought you out of Egypt." In the same way, the Christian life doesn't start with a list of dos and don'ts. It starts with the gospel, with what God has already done for us in Jesus. Obedience is our response to grace, not our attempt to earn it.

Second, loving God means loving him with everything. The command isn't "love God with part of your heart" or "love God when it's convenient." It's all your heart, all your soul, all your strength. That kind of love touches every part of life: how you spend your time, how you treat people, what you think about when nobody's watching. It's not just a feeling. It's a direction for your whole life.

Third, faith has to be passed on deliberately. Moses didn't assume the next generation would pick up faith by accident. He commanded parents to talk about God constantly, to weave the story of redemption into everyday conversation. Faith doesn't transfer through osmosis. It transfers through intentional, daily, honest teaching in the home.

Fourth, prosperity is a spiritual test. It's easy to trust God when you're desperate. The harder test is trusting him when everything is going well, when your life is comfortable and you start to think you don't need him as much. Moses saw this coming from a mile away. He warned them because he knew: a full stomach can produce an empty heart.

Fifth, when someone asks why you live the way you do, tell the story. Moses didn't say, "Give them a list of rules." He said, "Tell them what God did." The best explanation of the Christian life isn't a moral argument. It's a story of rescue.

TALKING POINTS

1. **The Ten Commandments begin with what God has done, not what God demands.** Why does this order matter?

How does it change the way you think about rules and obedience?

2. **The command to love God with all your heart, soul, and strength is total and absolute.** What do you think it looks like practically for someone your age to love God with "all your strength"?

3. **Moses told parents to talk about God "when you sit at home, when you walk along the road, when you lie down, and when you get up."** What would it look like if your family talked about God that naturally? What gets in the way?

4. **Moses warned that prosperity could make people forget God.** Do you think that's true today? How can someone enjoy good things without letting those things push God to the side?

5. **When a child asks, "Why do we follow these commands?" the answer Moses gives is a story, not a lecture.** Why is a story more powerful than a list of rules?

Moses has laid the foundation. He's given the people the commandments that define their relationship with God, and he's given them the one sentence that captures the heart of it all: love the Lord your God with everything you have.

But knowing what to do and actually doing it are two different things. The land ahead is full of temptations, and Moses knows exactly how easy it will be for the people to drift. So he's about to get very specific about the dangers waiting for them and how to stay faithful when everything around them is pulling them away.

Turn the page.

3

NOT BECAUSE OF YOU

There's a scene in Disney's *Dumbo* that changes everything. For most of the film, Dumbo is a joke. He's a baby elephant with ears so enormous they drag on the ground. The other elephants are embarrassed by him. The circus ringmaster turns him into a clown. Nobody sees anything special in him. He's small, he's strange, and he definitely doesn't look like somebody destined for greatness.

Then, through a wild turn of events, Dumbo discovers he can fly. Those ridiculous ears, the ones everybody laughed at, turn out to be wings. But here's the catch: Dumbo doesn't believe he can do it on his own. His friend Timothy Mouse gives him a "magic feather" and tells him to hold it while he flies. Dumbo clutches that feather like his life depends on it, and up he goes.

It works. Until it doesn't. Mid-flight, the feather slips from his grip and spirals away. Dumbo panics. He starts to plummet. And Timothy screams from his hat, "The feather was a fake! You can fly! You can fly!"

It's a great movie moment. But when I read Deuteronomy 7–11, I think Moses is delivering the opposite message.

He's not telling Israel, "You had it in you all along." He's saying something much more humbling: "You didn't have it in you at all. Everything you have, everything you are, everything you'll ever accomplish in that land across the Jordan, is because of God. Not because of you."

These five chapters are Moses' most sustained and passionate warning against the most dangerous thing that can happen to God's people: forgetting who got them here.

THE SMALLEST OF ALL PEOPLES

Moses starts chapter 7 by addressing the elephant in the room. Israel is about to enter a land occupied by seven nations that are bigger, stronger, and better established than they are. The cities are fortified. The armies are experienced. The odds are not in Israel's favor.

But God promises to go before them. He will drive out the nations. He will hand them over. He will fight for his people. The victories over Sihon and Og were just a preview. If God could handle two powerful kings east of the Jordan, these Canaanite kingdoms don't stand a chance.

Then Moses pauses and says something the Israelites need to hear more than anything: "The Lord did not set his affection on you and choose you because you were more numerous than other peoples, for you were the fewest of all peoples. But it was because the Lord loved you and kept the oath he swore to your forefathers that he brought you out with a mighty hand and redeemed you from the land of slavery."

Read that again. God didn't choose Israel because they were impressive. They were the *least* impressive. They weren't the biggest nation, the most powerful civilization, or the most morally upright people on earth. God chose them for one reason: because he loved them. Period. And because he had made a promise to Abraham, Isaac, and Jacob that he intended to keep.

This is one of the most important ideas in the entire Bible. God's love is not a reward for being lovable. It's a choice he makes freely, aimed at people who haven't earned it and can't claim credit for it. That's grace. And it's the foundation on which everything else in these chapters rests.

Moses also warns them sternly about what to do when they arrive: tear down the pagan altars, smash the idols, and don't intermarry with the people of the land. This isn't ethnic hostility. Moses is concerned that if the Israelites start mixing their worship with the local religions, they'll be pulled away from the God who rescued them. The issue isn't the people. The issue is the gods. Idolatry is contagious, and Moses knows it.

NOT BY BREAD ALONE

Chapter 8 may be the most relevant chapter in Deuteronomy for anyone living a comfortable life. And it begins with a memory. "Remember how the Lord your God led you all the way in the desert these forty years, to humble you and to test you in order to know what was in your heart."

God had a purpose for those wilderness years. He wasn't just punishing the previous generation. He was teaching this one. He let them get hungry, and then he fed them with manna, bread from heaven that appeared fresh on the ground every morning. Why? "To teach you that man does not live on bread alone but on every word that comes from the mouth of the Lord."

This is the verse Jesus quoted when Satan tempted him in the wilderness. It's one of the most important sentences in the Old Testament. Physical food keeps your body alive, but it's God's word that sustains your whole life. The manna was proof: God can provide in ways you never expected, but only if you trust him.

Moses then paints a gorgeous picture of the land they're about to enter: streams and pools, wheat and barley, vines and fig trees, pomegranates and olives and honey. Iron in the rocks. Copper in the hills. They will eat and be satisfied. They will build fine houses and settle down. Their flocks will grow, and their silver and gold will multiply.

And then Moses drops the warning like a hammer. "When you have eaten and are satisfied, when you build fine houses and settle down, and when your herds and flocks grow large and your silver and gold increase, then your heart will become proud and you will forget the Lord your God, who brought you out of Egypt, out of the land of slavery."

He's describing a downward spiral: fullness leads to forgetfulness, forgetfulness leads to pride, and pride leads to a devastating lie. "You may say to yourself, 'My power and the strength of my hands have produced this wealth for me.'"

That lie is the root of all idolatry. It's the moment you stop seeing your life as a gift and start seeing it as an achievement. It's the moment you replace gratitude with self-congratulation. And Moses says it will destroy them just as surely as it destroyed the nations before them.

The antidote? "Remember the Lord your God, for it is he who gives you the ability to produce wealth." Even your *ability* to work hard and succeed is a gift. God is the source of every-thing, and the moment you forget that, you're already on the road to ruin.

STIFF-NECKED

If chapter 8 warns against pride in the future, chapter 9 demolishes pride in the present. Moses turns to his people and says, essentially, "Let me make something crystal clear: you are not getting this land because you deserve it."

"Do not say to yourself, 'The Lord has brought me here to take possession of this land because of my righteousness.' No! It is on account of the wickedness of these nations that the Lord is going to drive them out before you. It is not because of your righteousness or your integrity that you are going in to possess their land."

Moses repeats this point three times in six verses, as if he can see them already rehearsing the wrong story. Then he makes it personal: "Understand, then, that it is not because of your righteousness that the Lord your God is giving you this good land to possess, for you are a stiff-necked people."

"Stiff-necked" is an image borrowed from farming. It de-scribes an ox that refuses to turn where the farmer is steering, that plants its feet and locks its neck against the yoke. That's Israel. Stubborn. Resistant. Constantly pulling in the wrong direction.

And then Moses proves it. He retells the story of the golden calf, the worst moment in Israel's history. While Moses was on the mountain receiving the covenant from God, the people below pressured Aaron into making an idol. Forty days. That's all it took for them to break the covenant they had just sworn to keep. God was so furious he told Moses, "Leave me alone, so that I may destroy them and blot out their name from under heaven."

Think about what that means. God was ready to end the entire nation and start over with Moses. The covenant, the promises, the whole plan, nearly collapsed because of one act of brazen idolatry.

But Moses interceded. He threw himself before God and prayed for forty days and forty nights, refusing to eat or drink. He reminded God of his promises to Abraham, Isaac, and Jacob. He appealed to God's reputation among the nations. And God listened. He relented. The covenant survived, not because of Israel's faithfulness, but because of Moses' prayer and God's mercy.

Moses also mentions, almost in passing, three other places where Israel rebelled: Taberah, where they complained and God sent fire; Massah, where they demanded water and tested God; and Kibroth Hattaavah, where they craved meat and God sent quail along with a plague. The pattern is relentless. Rebellion after rebellion after rebellion. And yet here they are, still alive, still God's people, still standing on the edge of the Promised Land.

That's grace. Not earned. Not deserved. Just given.

WHAT DOES THE LORD REQUIRE?

After tearing down every possible basis for Israelite pride, Moses rebuilds on the only foundation that matters: God's character.

In chapter 10, Moses asks one of the most important questions in the Bible: "And now, Israel, what does the Lord your God ask of you?"

His answer is stunning in its simplicity: "To fear the Lord your God, to walk in all his ways, to love him, to serve the Lord your God with all your heart and with all your soul, and to keep the commands of the Lord."

That's it. Fear. Walk. Love. Serve. Keep. Not because you're trying to earn God's favor, but because he's already given it. The response to grace isn't self-congratulation. It's devotion.

Then Moses says something unexpected: "Circumcise your hearts, and do not be stiff-necked any longer." Physical circumcision was the outward sign of belonging to God's covenant people. But Moses says the outward sign isn't enough. God wants the inside to match the outside. He wants soft hearts, not just marked bodies. He wants people who are genuinely transformed, not just going through the motions.

And then Moses describes who this God is. He is the God of gods and Lord of lords, great and mighty and awesome. He shows no favoritism and accepts no bribes. He defends the fatherless and the widow. He loves the foreigner, providing food and clothing.

That last detail matters. The God of the universe, the one who owns the heavens and the earth and everything in them, pays attention to the people nobody else notices: orphans, widows, immigrants. And because God loves the vulnerable, Moses says, "You are to love those who are foreigners, for you yourselves were foreigners in Egypt."

If you want to know what loving God looks like in everyday life, Deuteronomy 10 says it looks like caring for people who can't repay you.

TWO MOUNTAINS, TWO PATHS

Moses wraps up this section in chapter 11 by laying out two clear paths. Obedience leads to blessing. Disobedience leads to curse. There is no third option.

He describes the land they're entering as fundamentally different from Egypt. In Egypt, they irrigated their crops by hand, hauling water from the Nile to their fields. But the Promised Land drinks rain from heaven. It depends on God for its water. The land itself is designed to keep them dependent on God, looking up instead of relying on their own effort.

And then Moses points to two mountains that will define the choice: Mount Gerizim and Mount Ebal. When the Israelites arrive in the land, they will stand between these peaks and hear the blessings pronounced from one and the curses from the other. The ceremony will make the choice physical and visible. Blessing on one side. Curse on the other. You have to pick a mountain.

This is the decision Moses has been building toward since chapter 5. Everything in these speeches has been leading to this moment: Will you remember or forget? Will you trust God or trust yourself? Will you love the Lord with everything you have, or will you drift toward the gods of comfort and self-sufficiency?

The choice is theirs. And it's ours.

WHAT THIS MEANS FOR US

First, God doesn't love you because you're impressive. He loves you because he loves you. That might sound circular, but it's the deepest truth in Scripture. You can't earn God's affection by being smarter, stronger, or better than everyone else. His love is a gift, not a trophy.

Second, success is the most dangerous test of faith. Moses didn't warn the Israelites about failure. He warned them about success. When everything is going well, when life is comfortable and the pantry is full, that's when you're most likely to forget God. The hardest prayer to pray isn't "Help me." It's "Thank you."

Third, your track record doesn't qualify you for God's grace. Israel's history was a disaster. Rebellion, idolatry, ingratitude, stubbornness, again and again. And yet God kept them. Grace isn't for people who have it together. It's for people who don't.

Fourth, what God requires is simpler than we make it. Fear him. Walk in his ways. Love him. Serve him. Keep his commands. That's the whole list. Not a complicated system. Not an impossible standard. Just a life pointed in the right direction, fueled by gratitude.

Fifth, loving God and loving vulnerable people are the same thing. You can't claim to fear the God who defends orphans and widows and then ignore the people around you who are struggling. The way you treat the overlooked and the powerless reveals what you really believe about God.

TALKING POINTS

1. **God chose Israel not because they were great but because he loved them.** How does it change your understanding of your relationship with God to know that his love isn't based on your performance?

2. **Moses warned that prosperity could lead to pride: "My power produced this wealth."** Where do you see this attitude in the world today? Have you ever caught yourself taking credit for something that was really a gift?

3. **The golden calf happened just forty days after Israel swore to obey God.** Why do you think people can make sincere promises to God and break them so quickly? What helps you stay faithful to commitments you've made?

4. **Moses told the Israelites to "circumcise your hearts."** What do you think it means to have a "soft heart" toward God versus a "stiff neck"? What's the difference between going through the motions and genuinely meaning it?

5. **God is described as defending the fatherless, the widow, and the foreigner.** Why do you think God pays special attention to vulnerable people? How can you follow his example this week?

Moses has now taken the people through the full arc: the story of where they've been, the heart of the covenant, and the warning against forgetting who they are. He's laid out two mountains and two paths.

Now comes the specific instructions. If the first half of Moses' sermon was about *why* to obey, the second half is about *how*. The laws are about to get detailed, practical, and surprisingly relevant, starting with where and how to worship the God who chose them.

Turn the page.

4

RULES FOR A FREE PEOPLE

Mark Twain's *Adventures of Huckleberry Finn* is about a boy who has to decide which rules are worth following.

Huck Finn lives in Missouri before the Civil War, in a society that runs on rules. Rules about how to dress, how to talk in church, how to behave at the dinner table. But the biggest rule, the one nobody questions, is that slavery is normal. Owning another human being is legal, respectable, and accepted by nearly everyone Huck has ever known. Helping a slave escape is a crime. In Huck's world, the "good" people are the ones who follow this rule, and the "bad" people are the ones who break it.

Then Huck meets Jim, a runaway slave, on an island in the Mississippi River. They build a raft and float south together, and somewhere along the way, Huck starts to see Jim not as somebody's property but as a person: a father who misses his children, a man who is loyal and kind, a friend who would risk his life for Huck without thinking twice.

And that creates a crisis. Everything Huck has been taught says he should turn Jim in. His conscience, shaped by the rules of his society, tells him that helping Jim escape is stealing and that he'll go to hell for it. At the most famous moment in the book, Huck holds a letter he's written to Jim's owner, ready to do the "right" thing. Then he thinks about Jim. He tears the letter up and says, "All right, then, I'll go to hell."

Huck chose the person over the rule. And the reason Twain's novel is so powerful is that every reader knows Huck made the right choice, even though every rule in his world said otherwise. The problem wasn't that Huck was lawless. The problem was that his society's laws were wicked.

That's the question Deuteronomy 12–18 answers from the opposite direction. What would it look like if a society's laws were actually *good*? What if the rules were written not by people protecting their own power, but by a God who cares about the powerless? What if the law didn't protect slave owners but freed slaves? What if it didn't entrench poverty but canceled debts? What if it didn't silence the vulnerable but gave them a voice?

That's exactly what these chapters describe. Not laws designed to crush people, but instructions for building the kind of society Huck Finn could only dream about: one where justice is real, worship is joyful, the poor are protected, and power answers to God.

ONE PLACE, ONE GOD

Moses begins this section with worship. Before he talks about courts or kings or anything else, he addresses how Israel will relate to God once they're settled in the land.

The first instruction is surprising: destroy every pagan

worship site in the land. Tear down the altars. Smash the sacred stones. Burn the carved images. Don't leave a trace of Canaanite religion standing.

This sounds harsh until you understand the context. Canaanite worship wasn't just a difference of opinion about religion. It involved practices that degraded human beings and dishonored the Creator. The altars and images weren't harmless decorations. They were gateways to a system of worship that would pull Israel away from the God who had rescued them. Moses knew that if they left the pagan shrines intact, it was only a matter of time before curiosity turned into compromise and compromise turned into full-blown idolatry.

In place of the scattered hilltop shrines of the Canaanites, God would establish one central place of worship. Moses calls it "the place the Lord your God will choose" to put his name. He doesn't name the location. That would come later. But the principle is clear: instead of worshiping wherever and however they pleased, the Israelites would gather in one place, at God's invitation, on God's terms.

And here's what's remarkable about that place: it wasn't a place of dread. It was a place of *celebration*. Moses describes worship as eating in God's presence, rejoicing over God's blessings, bringing gifts and offerings with glad hearts. Seven times in chapter 12, he uses the word "there," painting a picture of a community gathered together to feast and celebrate before the God who had given them everything.

This isn't the cold, dreary, rule-bound religion that some people imagine when they think of the Old Testament. This is a party. A feast. A family reunion in the presence of the living

God. And everyone was invited: sons and daughters, servants, and even the Levites who had no land of their own.

PROTECTING THE HEART

Chapter 13 takes a sharp turn. Having described the joy of true worship, Moses now addresses the most serious threat to it: people who try to lure Israel away from God.

He describes three scenarios, and each one is more personal than the last. First, a prophet or dreamer might perform a sign or wonder and then say, "Let's follow other gods." Even if the sign comes true, Moses says, don't listen. God is testing your loyalty. A miracle doesn't validate a message if the message contradicts what God has already said.

Second, a close family member, a brother or sister, a spouse, a best friend, might secretly try to pull you toward other gods. Moses says this is just as dangerous as a false prophet, maybe more so, because it comes from someone you love and trust.

Third, an entire town might go off the rails, abandoning the Lord to worship false gods.

In each case, the response Moses prescribes is severe. The seriousness of the consequences reflects the seriousness of the threat. Idolatry wasn't a minor infraction in Israel. It was treason against the King of the universe, a betrayal of the God who had personally rescued them from slavery. Moses is trying to protect the very thing that makes Israel *Israel*: their exclusive relationship with the one true God.

HOLY IN THE ORDINARY

Chapter 14 moves from the dramatic to the everyday. Moses

addresses something as basic as food: what the Israelites could and couldn't eat.

He opens with a stunning declaration: "You are the children of the Lord your God." That's the reason behind the food laws. Israel's identity as God's holy people wasn't meant to show up only at festivals and sacrifices. It was supposed to touch every corner of life, right down to the dinner table. Every meal was a reminder: you belong to God. You are set apart. Even the way you eat tells a story about who you are.

Moses also gives detailed instructions about the tithe, the practice of setting aside a tenth of their produce each year. But here's what's fascinating: in Deuteronomy, the tithe isn't a tax. It's a feast. The Israelites were to take their tithe to the central place of worship and eat it there, in the presence of God, with their families. It was a celebration of God's provision, and Moses specifically commands them to include the Levites and the poor who lived among them. Nobody was to be left out of the party.

NO POOR AMONG YOU

Chapter 15 contains some of the most radical economic legislation in the ancient world. Every seven years, all debts were to be canceled. Not reduced. Not renegotiated. Wiped clean. If your neighbor owed you money and the seventh year arrived, the debt was gone. Moses called it "the Lord's time for canceling debts."

Then he makes a statement that sounds almost impossible: "There need be no poor among you, for in the land the Lord your God is giving you to possess as your inheritance, he will richly bless you, if only you fully obey the Lord your God."

Moses wasn't naïve. He knew poverty wouldn't vanish overnight. A few verses later he says, "There will always be poor people in the land." But the point isn't that poverty is inevitable and there's nothing you can do about it. The point is that in a society shaped by God's values, *systemic, permanent poverty doesn't have to exist.* If people obey God's commands, if the rich are generous and debts are regularly forgiven, then nobody has to stay trapped at the bottom forever.

Moses even anticipates the objection. He knows that as the seventh year approaches, people will be tempted to stop lending because they won't get their money back. "Be careful," he warns, "that you do not harbor this wicked thought: 'The seventh year is near,' so that you show ill will toward your needy neighbor and give nothing." He calls stinginess a *sin.*

The same principle extends to servants. If someone had sold themselves into service because of debt, they were to be released after six years, and not sent away empty-handed. The master was to load them up with grain, wine, and livestock, enough to give them a fresh start. Why? "Remember that you were slaves in Egypt and the Lord your God redeemed you." You were broke once. God rescued you. Now do the same for the person standing in front of you.

THREE FEASTS AND FOUR OFFICES

Chapter 16 prescribes three annual festivals that would structure Israel's entire year around the memory of what God had done.

The Passover came first, a reenactment of the night God delivered Israel from Egypt. Every household would slaughter a lamb and eat it together, remembering the blood on the doorframes and the angel of death passing over. Then came the Festival of Weeks, seven weeks after Passover, a harvest celebration in which the people gave thanks for God's provision and shared their abundance with the Levites, the foreigners, the orphans, and the widows. Finally, the Festival of Booths came in the fall, when the people built temporary shelters and lived in them for a week, remembering the wilderness years when God sustained them with nothing but manna and a cloud.

Three festivals. Three memories. Three opportunities every year to stop and remember: we were slaves, God set us free, and everything we have is a gift.

Starting in the second half of chapter 16 and running through chapter 18, Moses outlines four offices that would govern Israel's community life: judges, kings, priests, and prophets.

Judges were to pursue "justice, only justice." No favoritism. No bribes. No twisting the law to benefit the powerful at the expense of the weak. The integrity of the courts was sacred, because in Israel, justice belonged to God.

The law of the king is especially striking. Moses anticipates that Israel will one day want a king "like all the nations around them." God permits it, but with severe restrictions. The king must not accumulate excessive horses (a symbol of military power), must not take many wives (which would pull his heart toward foreign gods), and must not hoard silver and gold. Instead, the king was to do one specific thing: write out a personal copy of God's law and read it every single day of his life, "so that he may learn to fear the Lord his God."

In other words, the king of Israel wasn't supposed to be above the law. He was supposed to be *under* it, just like everyone else. His job wasn't to rule by his own wisdom but to be shaped by God's word. That was a revolutionary concept in the ancient world, where kings were often considered divine or at least answerable to no one.

The priests, from the tribe of Levi, received no land inheritance. Instead, God himself was their inheritance. They were set apart to serve at the central place of worship, to teach the people God's law, and to stand in God's presence on behalf of the nation. The community was responsible for providing for them, sharing the offerings and tithes so the priests could focus on their calling.

Finally, Moses addresses prophets. The nations around Israel used diviners, sorcerers, and mediums to try to discover the will of the gods. Moses forbids all of it. Instead, God promises to raise up prophets like Moses, people who would speak God's word directly to the people. "I will put my words in his mouth," God says, "and he will tell them everything I command him."

This promise is one of the most important in Deuteronomy. It means God will never leave his people without a voice. He will keep speaking, keep guiding, keep sending messengers to call his people back when they drift. The line of prophets that followed Moses, from Samuel to Elijah to Isaiah to Jeremiah, fulfilled this promise generation after generation. And when Jesus arrived, Peter stood up in the temple and pointed to this very passage: "Moses said, 'The Lord your God will raise up for you a prophet like me from among your own people; you must listen to everything he tells you'" (Acts 3:22).

WHAT THIS MEANS FOR US

First, worship is meant to be joyful. The picture of worship in Deuteronomy 12 isn't solemn silence in a dark room. It's a feast, a celebration, a community gathered in the presence of a generous God. If your experience of worship feels dry and lifeless, Deuteronomy says that's not how it was designed. God invites his people into his presence to rejoice.

Second, generosity toward the poor isn't optional. The debt laws and servant laws of chapter 15 aren't suggestions for nice people. They're covenant obligations. God's people are supposed to be the most generous community on earth, because they've received the most generous gift imaginable: rescue from slavery by a God who owed them nothing.

Third, power must be accountable. Even the king of Israel was expected to read God's word daily and submit to it. No leader in God's community is above the law. The moment a leader stops being shaped by God's word, they've stopped being qualified to lead.

Fourth, God keeps speaking. The promise of prophets like Moses means God doesn't go silent. He keeps raising up voices to call his people back, to apply his word to new situations, and to point forward to the one who was coming. That promise reaches its ultimate fulfillment in Jesus, the prophet, priest, and king who embodies everything these chapters describe.

TALKING POINTS

1. **Deuteronomy describes worship as eating, celebrating, and rejoicing in God's presence.** How does that compare

with your experience of worship? What would it look like to approach God with that kind of joy?

2. **Moses said debts should be canceled every seven years and servants should be freed after six.** What do these laws reveal about God's values? How should they shape the way Christians think about money, debt, and generosity?

3. **The king of Israel was required to write out and read God's law every day.** Why do you think this was so important? What difference does it make when a leader is personally shaped by God's word?

4. **God told Israel not to use divination, sorcery, or mediums but instead to listen to his prophets.** Why do you think people are drawn to supernatural shortcuts instead of trusting God's revealed word?

5. **Moses said, "There need be no poor among you."** Do you think that's an achievable goal or an impossible ideal? What would a community look like that truly lived by this principle?

Moses has laid out the architecture of a just society: how to worship, how to handle money, how to lead, and how to listen for God's voice. But the laws aren't finished yet. There's still more to say about how a holy people should treat each other in the messy, complicated details of everyday life.

Turn the page.

5

WHAT LOVE LOOKS LIKE

Disney's *The Hunchback of Notre Dame* tells the story of a young man named Quasimodo who has been locked in a bell tower his entire life.

His guardian, Judge Claude Frollo, has convinced him that the world outside is dangerous and cruel, that ordinary people would reject Quasimodo because of his appearance. Frollo presents himself as compassionate, the only person who cares about this deformed bell-ringer. But the truth is exactly the opposite. Frollo is the cruel one. He uses religion and law as weapons to control Quasimodo and to terrorize the Romani people living in Paris. He burns houses, arrests the innocent, and justifies it all as righteousness. His rules aren't designed to protect people. They're designed to protect *his* power.

When Quasimodo finally leaves the tower and enters the world, he discovers something Frollo never wanted him to know: ordinary people can be kind. The outsiders Frollo despised turn out to be warm, generous, and brave. And the system of "justice" Frollo enforced turns out to be nothing but dressed-up cruelty.

The contrast between Frollo's version of law and the actual justice Quasimodo discovers is striking. And it's the same contrast you'll notice when you read Deuteronomy 19–26. These chapters are filled with laws, dozens of them, covering everything from courtroom procedures to bird nests. But unlike Frollo's rules, these laws aren't designed to crush people or protect the powerful. They're designed to protect the powerless. They're what love looks like when it gets practical.

JUSTICE THAT PROTECTS

Moses opens this section with a system designed to prevent a specific kind of injustice: the killing of an innocent person in the heat of revenge.

In the ancient world, if someone killed your relative, your family had the right, even the duty, to hunt down the killer and execute them. This was called "blood vengeance," and the family member who carried it out was called the "avenger of blood." The problem was obvious: what if the killing was an accident? What if a man was chopping wood and the axehead flew off the handle and struck his neighbor? That's a tragedy, not a murder. But a grieving family might not stop to ask questions.

God's solution was the cities of refuge. Three cities were to be set apart in the Promised Land, with well-maintained roads leading to them, so that anyone who accidentally caused a death could flee there and be safe until a fair trial could determine what happened. If the killing was genuinely accidental, the person could stay in the city and live. If it was murder, the killer would be handed over for execution.

This system accomplished something remarkable: it slowed down the cycle of violence long enough for justice to happen. It protected the innocent from rash vengeance while still ensuring that murderers faced consequences. Mercy and justice, working together.

Moses also addresses the courtroom itself. No one could be convicted of a crime on the testimony of a single witness. Two or three witnesses were required. And if someone was caught lying in court, they would receive the same punishment the accused would have received. Perjury wasn't just frowned upon. It was treated as one of the most dangerous threats to a just society, because if the courts can't be trusted, nobody is safe.

RULES FOR THE BATTLEFIELD

Chapter 20 turns to warfare, and the instructions are surprisingly humane for the ancient world.

Before any battle, a priest was to address the army with words of encouragement: "Do not be fainthearted or afraid. The Lord your God is the one who goes with you to fight for you." This wasn't just a pep talk. It was a theological statement: the outcome of the battle belongs to God, not to the size of your army.

Then came a series of exemptions that would have shocked any military commander in the ancient Near East. If a soldier had just built a new house and hadn't moved in yet, he could go home. If he had just planted a vineyard and hadn't eaten its fruit, he could go home. If he had just gotten engaged and hadn't married yet, he could go home. And if anyone was simply afraid, he could go home too, so his fear wouldn't spread to the others.

Think about what this says about God's values. Military efficiency wasn't the highest priority. People were. A man's home, his livelihood, his marriage, and even his emotional well-being mattered more than filling the ranks. God would fight for Israel regardless of their numbers. What he cared about was the kind of people they were, not the size of their army.

Moses also drew a line around how far warfare could go. When besieging a city, the Israelites were forbidden from cutting down fruit trees. "Is the tree your enemy?" Moses asks. Even in war, creation deserved respect. You don't destroy what sustains life, even the life of your enemies.

THE DIGNITY OF EVERY PERSON

Chapters 21–25 cover an enormous range of topics that might seem random at first glance. But underneath the variety runs a single thread: every person has dignity, and God's laws exist to protect it.

If a dead body was found in a field between two towns and nobody knew who was responsible, the elders of the nearest town had to perform a solemn ceremony to declare their innocence and ask God to cleanse the land of the guilt. Even an unsolved death couldn't be shrugged off. Every life mattered enough to demand a response.

If a soldier took a captive woman as his wife, she was to be given time to grieve for her family before the marriage. And if the man later decided he didn't want her, he had to let her go free. He couldn't sell her or treat her as property. Even in the brutal context of ancient warfare, God insisted on a baseline of dignity for women.

If you saw your neighbor's ox or donkey wandering loose, you couldn't just walk past. You had to bring it back. If you saw a bird's nest with a mother sitting on her eggs, you could take the eggs, but you had to let the mother go. If you built a new house, you had to put a railing around the roof so nobody would fall off. These aren't grand theological statements. They're small, practical instructions that add up to a big idea: pay attention to the world around you and take responsibility for the well-being of others, even in small things.

The laws about honest business are just as pointed. You couldn't have two sets of weights in your bag, one heavy and one light, to cheat people in the marketplace. "The Lord your God detests anyone who does these things, anyone who deals dishonestly," Moses says. Cheating in business wasn't just bad manners. It was an offense against the God who rescued you and called you to be different from the nations around you.

THE ONES NOBODY NOTICES

If there's one group of people Deuteronomy cares about more than any other, it's the vulnerable: the widow, the orphan, and the foreigner.

These three categories come up again and again throughout chapters 19–26. When you harvest your field, don't go back for the sheaf you missed. Leave it for the foreigner, the orphan, and the widow. When you beat your olive trees, don't go over the branches twice. Leave what remains. When you gather grapes, don't pick the vineyard clean. Leave some behind.

This practice, called gleaning, was God's welfare system for ancient Israel. It wasn't charity handed down from above. It was an opportunity for the poor to work and feed themselves with dignity, while the landowners demonstrated that their abundance wasn't really theirs to hoard. Everything came from God, and some of it was meant to be shared.

Moses gives the reason for these laws in a phrase that echoes throughout the book: "Remember that you were slaves in Egypt." You know what it feels like to be powerless. You know what it's like to have nothing. Don't forget where you came from, and don't let anyone in your community experience what you experienced.

When you lend your neighbor something and he gives you his cloak as collateral, you have to return it before sunset so he has something to sleep in. When you hire a worker, you have to pay him before the sun goes down, because he's counting on that money to feed his family that night. "Do not take advantage of a hired worker who is poor and needy, whether that worker is a fellow Israelite or a foreigner living in one of your towns."

Did you catch that? The foreigner gets the same protection as the Israelite. In a world where foreigners were routinely exploited, enslaved, or ignored, God's law said: treat them the same. Their vulnerability doesn't make them less human. It makes them more deserving of your care.

TELLING THE STORY ONE MORE TIME

Chapter 26 brings the entire law section to a close with one of the most beautiful rituals in the Old Testament: the offering of firstfruits.

When the Israelites finally settled in the land and harvested their first crops, they were to take the very first portion of the harvest, put it in a basket, carry it to the place God had chosen, and present it to the priest with a declaration. And that declaration was a story:

"My father was a wandering Aramean, and he went down into Egypt with a few people and lived there and became a great nation, powerful and numerous. But the Egyptians mistreated us and made us suffer, subjecting us to harsh labor. Then we cried out to the Lord, the God of our ancestors, and the Lord heard our voice and saw our misery, toil, and oppression. So the Lord brought us out of Egypt with a mighty hand and an outstretched arm, with great terror and with signs and wonders. He brought us to this place and gave us this land, a land flowing with milk and honey; and now I bring the firstfruits of the soil that you, Lord, have given me."

Every year, every Israelite farmer would stand before God and retell the story of redemption. Not someone else's story. *Their* story. "We were slaves. God heard us. God rescued us. God brought us here. And this basket of grain is proof that he keeps his promises."

This is how the law section ends. Not with a rule but with a ritual of gratitude. Not with a command but with a confession. After all the detailed instructions about courts and warfare and business and marriage and farming, Moses brings everything back to the one thing that holds it all together: the story of a God who saw suffering, heard cries, and acted.

The chapter closes with a mutual declaration. God affirms that Israel is his treasured people, and Israel affirms that the Lord is their God. The covenant relationship is sealed. The obligations have been spelled out. And the purpose of it all is declared: that Israel would be "a people holy to the Lord your God," set high above the nations "in praise, fame, and honor."

Not for their own glory. For his.

WHAT THIS MEANS FOR US

First, justice and mercy belong together. The cities of refuge show that a just society doesn't choose between protecting victims and protecting the innocent accused. It does both. Whenever justice is practiced without mercy, or mercy without justice, something has gone wrong.

Second, the small stuff matters. Returning a neighbor's lost animal, building a railing on your roof, paying a worker on time, leaving grain in the field for the poor. These aren't dramatic acts of heroism. They're everyday choices that reveal whether you actually love your neighbor or just talk about it. Love gets practical, or it isn't love.

Third, how you treat the powerless reveals who you really are. A society's character isn't measured by how it treats the rich and powerful. It's measured by how it treats the widow, the orphan, the foreigner, and the worker who lives paycheck to paycheck. God watches how his people treat the people nobody else is watching out for.

Fourth, gratitude is the engine of obedience. The first-fruits ritual didn't start with "here's what you owe God." It started with "here's what God did for you." Every act of obedience in Deuteronomy flows from remembering the story of rescue. When gratitude dies, obedience becomes drudgery. When gratitude is alive, even the smallest commandment becomes an act of worship.

TALKING POINTS

1. **The cities of refuge were designed to prevent revenge killings by slowing things down and allowing for a fair trial.** Why is it so important to resist acting on anger and instead wait for the truth to come out? Can you think of a time when jumping to conclusions caused harm?

2. **Soldiers who had just built a house, planted a vineyard, or gotten engaged were sent home from battle.** What does this tell you about what God values? How does this compare with what our culture considers most important?

3. **The gleaning laws required farmers to leave part of their harvest for the poor. This let the poor work for their food with dignity rather than simply receiving a handout.** Why do you think dignity matters so much in how we help others?

4. **Moses repeatedly says, "Remember that you were slaves in Egypt" as the reason for treating others well.** How does remembering your own hard times make you more compassionate toward others who are struggling?

5. **The firstfruits offering involved retelling the story of God's rescue every single year.** Why do you think repeating the story matters? What stories of God's faithfulness do you need to keep telling?

Moses has finished laying out the laws. Every corner of life has been addressed: worship, leadership, justice, warfare, family, business, and care for the poor. The vision is stunning—an entire society shaped by the character of the God who rescued it.

But will they do it? Moses knows the answer, and he's about to lay out the consequences with devastating clarity. Two paths lie ahead: one leads to blessing beyond imagination, and the other leads to a darkness Israel can barely comprehend.

Turn the page.

6

TWO MOUNTAINS, TWO FUTURES

George Orwell wrote a book called *Animal Farm* about a group of animals who stage a revolution. The animals on Manor Farm are miserable. Their human owner, Mr. Jones, works them hard, feeds them little, and takes everything they produce. So one day, led by the pigs, the animals rise up, chase Jones off the farm, and take over. They paint their new rules on the barn wall: "All animals are equal." They rename the place Animal Farm and set out to build a society where everyone shares the work and the rewards. For a while, it's wonderful. The harvest is better than ever. The animals sing and celebrate. Freedom tastes like everything they hoped it would be.

But then things start to change. The pigs, who are the smartest animals, gradually begin taking more food, making more decisions, and working less. They move into the farmhouse. They start sleeping in beds. They change the rules, one by one, always with a reasonable-sounding excuse. The other animals have a vague feeling that something is wrong, but they can't quite put their hooves on what it is. By the end of the story, the pigs are walking on two legs, wearing clothes, and carrying whips. The final scene is devastating: the other animals look through the farmhouse window at the pigs sitting with human farmers, and they can't tell the difference between the pigs and the men. The revolution has come full circle. The liberated have become the oppressors.

Orwell's point is devastating: freedom that forgets its own principles will always destroy itself.

That's exactly what Moses is warning about in Deuteronomy 27–28. These two chapters lay out the most vivid picture of two possible futures in the entire Bible. One path leads to a life so blessed that the nations of the earth will look at Israel in awe. The other leads to a horror so complete that the freed slaves end up back in chains, unable to tell the difference between their new reality and the Egypt they escaped.

Two mountains. Two paths. And the choice is theirs.

STONES, ALTARS, AND A CEREMONY

Chapter 27 begins with instructions for something Israel has never done before: a ceremony that will take place the moment they arrive in the Promised Land.

When the Israelites cross the Jordan, Moses tells them, they are to set up large stones, coat them with plaster, and write on them the entire law that Moses has been teaching. Then they are to build an altar of uncut stones on Mount Ebal and offer sacrifices to God. Whole burnt offerings and peace offerings, the same kinds of sacrifices that sealed the covenant at Sinai. And then they are to eat together in the presence of God and rejoice.

This matters more than it might seem at first. The covenant between God and Israel had been made at Mount Sinai, in the wilderness, on foreign soil. The land of Canaan wasn't part of the deal yet, because they weren't in it yet. But now, finally, they're about to cross over. The ceremony on Mount Ebal would bring the land itself into the covenant relationship. God, people, and land would finally be together, just as he had promised Abraham centuries earlier.

The inscribed stones served as a public record, a monument declaring that this land now belonged to God's covenant people and that God's law governed life within it. The altar and the feast celebrated the moment. And the act of writing the law clearly on the stones for everyone to see was itself a statement: this law is not hidden or secret. It's public. It's accessible. It belongs to everyone.

Then Moses describes something dramatic. The twelve tribes are to divide into two groups. Six tribes will stand on Mount Gerizim, and six will stand on Mount Ebal. These two mountains face each other across a narrow valley near the ancient city of Shechem, the very place where God first appeared to Abraham when he entered the land and promised, "To your offspring I will give this land." The Levites will stand in the valley between the mountains and read out a series of curses, and after each one, all the people will respond: "Amen."

The twelve curses target specific sins, many of them hidden: making idols in secret, dishonoring your parents, moving your neighbor's boundary marker, misleading the blind, withholding justice from the vulnerable, sexual sins, and secret murder. The common thread is that these are offenses committed behind closed doors, where no human court would catch you.

The point is powerful: God sees what people do in the dark. You might escape human justice, but you will never escape his.

THE BLESSINGS

Chapter 28 opens with what might be the most beautiful conditional promise in the Bible. "If you fully obey the Lord your God and carefully follow all his commands I give you today, the Lord your God will set you high above all the nations on earth."

What follows is a cascade of blessings, six statements that cover every dimension of life. Blessed in the city. Blessed in the country. Blessed in your children, your crops, your livestock. Blessed when you come in and blessed when you go out. God will defeat your enemies. He will bless your storehouses and everything you put your hand to. He will establish you as his holy people, and all the nations of the earth will see that you are called by his name and will stand in awe.

The rain will come at the right time. The harvests will overflow. You will lend to many nations but borrow from none. You will be the head, not the tail. You will always be on top and never on the bottom.

It's a vision of life as God designed it: a people thriving in a good land, living under his blessing, radiating his character to the watching world. It's not a prosperity gospel in the modern sense. It's not "obey God and get rich." It's the picture of what happens when a whole society operates the way God intended: worship is joyful, justice is real, the poor are cared for, and the land itself responds to the faithfulness of its people.

But the blessings come with a condition. "If you fully obey." Not partially. Not when it's convenient. Not when you feel like it. The blessings are not automatic rewards dropped into a vending machine. They're the natural fruit of a life aligned with the God who created everything. And the moment that alignment breaks, so does the blessing.

THE CURSES

Then the tone shifts. And it shifts hard. "However, if you do not obey the Lord your God and do not carefully follow all his commands and decrees I give you today, all these curses will come on you and overtake you."

The curse section is five times longer than the blessings. That's not because God is more interested in punishment than reward. It's because Moses is a preacher making a final appeal. He knows his people. He knows how easily they drift. He's piling up the warnings because the stakes are unimaginably high, and he wants them to feel the weight of what disobedience will cost.

The curses begin as a mirror image of the blessings, reversing every promise: cursed in the city, cursed in the country, cursed in your basket and your kneading trough, cursed when you come in and cursed when you go out. Everything that was blessed is now broken.

Then Moses goes further. Disease will strike. Drought will scorch the land. The sky will become bronze and the ground will become iron. Enemies will defeat you and scatter you, and your dead bodies will be food for the birds and no one will frighten them away. The plagues of Egypt, the very horrors God once inflicted on your oppressors, will come back on you. You will plant but not harvest. You will build but not live in what you build. You will be engaged but someone else will marry her.

The curses escalate relentlessly. Foreigners will rise above you while you sink lower and lower. They will be the head; you will be the tail. A nation you've never heard of will swoop down like an eagle and besiege your cities until the walls fall. The siege will be so severe that desperate people will resort to horrors too terrible to describe, things Moses barely hints at but that history would later confirm in gruesome detail during the Babylonian and Roman sieges of Jerusalem.

And then the ultimate reversal. The people God brought out of Egypt will go back. "The Lord will send you back in ships to Egypt on a journey I said you should never make again. There you will offer yourselves for sale to your enemies as male and female slaves, but no one will buy you."

That last line might be the most devastating sentence in the Old Testament. You'll try to sell yourselves back into slavery, and nobody will even want you. The nation that was set "high above all the nations" will sink so low that it has no value even as property.

WHY SO MUCH DARKNESS?

You might be wondering: why would Moses say all this? Why would God include this in the Bible? Is he trying to scare people into obedience?

In a sense, yes. But not in a cruel way. Moses is doing what any loving parent does when their child is about to do something dangerous: he's making absolutely sure they understand the consequences before they choose.

Everything in these curses is conditional. Nothing here is fated or inevitable. Moses isn't predicting the future. He's describing what *will* happen *if*. The whole point is to make the choice so vivid, so stark, so undeniable, that nobody can later say, "We didn't know."

And the curses aren't random punishments dreamed up by an angry God. They're the natural unraveling of a life cut off from the source of life. When Israel abandons the God who rescued them, they don't just lose a few perks. They lose everything, because everything they have came from him in the first place. The blessings were never their own achievement. They were gifts. And when you reject the Giver, you lose the gifts.

What makes this chapter truly sobering is that history proved every word of it true. The northern kingdom fell to Assyria in 722 BC. The southern kingdom fell to Babylon in 586 BC. The temple was destroyed. The people were carried into exile. The curses Moses described, disease, siege, starvation, scattering among the nations, all of it happened, exactly as he warned, centuries later.

The prophet Daniel, writing from exile in Babylon, acknowledged it plainly: "Just as it is written in the Law of Moses, all this disaster has come upon us." The covenant wasn't broken by God. It was broken by his people. And the curses that fell were the fine print they had agreed to.

But even here, the story doesn't end in darkness. Moses had already hinted in chapter 4 that even after the worst-case scenario, if the people returned to God with all their hearts, he would not abandon them. The covenant curses were real, but so was God's mercy. Judgment was never meant to be the last word.

WHAT THIS MEANS FOR US

First, choices have real consequences. This chapter refuses to let us live in a fantasy where our decisions don't matter. They do. The path of faithfulness leads somewhere, and the path of rebellion leads somewhere else. Moses lays both roads out in blinding clarity so that nobody has to guess.

Second, blessing is never something we earn; it's something we receive. The blessings of chapter 28 aren't wages for good behavior. They're the fruit of a relationship with God. When we walk in his ways, we align ourselves with the way life was designed to work. When we don't, things fall apart, not because God is vindictive, but because we've disconnected from the source.

Third, God's warnings are an act of love. A God who didn't care wouldn't bother warning you. The length and intensity of the curses reflect the depth of Moses' pastoral concern, and behind it, the depth of God's desire that his people would choose life. Every terrifying word is an invitation to turn the other way.

Fourth, the gospel shines brightest against a dark backdrop. Paul wrote that "Christ redeemed us from the curse of the law by becoming a curse for us" (Galatians 3:13). Jesus took the weight of the covenant curse on himself so that the blessing promised to Abraham could reach the whole world. Deuteronomy 28 makes the cross necessary, and makes the cross make sense.

TALKING POINTS

1. **The ceremony at Ebal and Gerizim made the choice between blessing and curse physically visible, with tribes**

standing on opposite mountains. Why do you think God wanted the people to *see* the choice, not just hear about it?

2. **The blessings cover every area of life: family, work, food, safety, reputation.** What does this tell you about how far God's interest in your life extends?

3. **The curse section is five times longer than the blessings.** Why do you think Moses spent so much more time on the warnings? What does that say about his understanding of human nature?

4. **Moses described the curses as the reversal of everything God had done for Israel, ending with a return to Egypt.** Why is it significant that disobedience doesn't just lead to something new and bad, but takes you back to where you started?

5. **Paul says Jesus "became a curse for us."** How does reading the curse section of Deuteronomy 28 change the way you understand what Jesus did on the cross?

Moses has shown his people both futures with unflinching honesty. The blessings are real. The curses are real. The choice is real. But he's not finished. He has one more appeal to make, one final moment where he'll look this generation in the eye and ask them to choose. And the words he's about to speak are some of the most powerful in the entire Bible.

Turn the page.

7

CHOOSE LIFE

There's a moment in Disney's *Pocahontas* where the entire story balances on a single decision. Pocahontas is paddling her canoe down a river when she reaches a fork. One path is smooth and steady, the familiar route she's always taken. The other path is wild, rushing with white water, heading somewhere she's never been. Her father wants her to take the safe path, to marry a warrior from their tribe and settle into a predictable life. But something inside Pocahontas knows she's being pulled in a different direction, toward something bigger and more uncertain.

She asks Grandmother Willow, the ancient tree who speaks wisdom, what to do. "Listen with your heart," the old tree says. "You will understand."

In the end, Pocahontas doesn't take the safe, predictable river. She chooses the unknown. And that choice changes everything, for her, for her people, and for the strangers who have just arrived on her shores.

What makes the scene powerful isn't the choice itself. It's the weight of it. Both paths are real. Both lead somewhere. And once she starts paddling, there's no turning back.

That's where we are in Deuteronomy 29–30. Moses has spent the entire book laying out two paths with total honesty: one leads to life and blessing, the other to death and curse. He's told the people their history, given them the law, warned them about the dangers ahead, and described both futures in vivid detail. Now, in his final sermon, he looks this generation in the eye and says the most important words in the whole book.

"I have set before you life and death, blessings and curses. Now choose life."

This is the moment everything has been building toward. The fork in the river. And the choice belongs to them.

EYES THAT FINALLY SEE

Moses opens his third and final sermon by gathering the entire nation, every last person, into one place. Not just the leaders. Not just the men. Everybody: tribal heads, elders, officials, all the men of Israel, the children, the wives, and even the foreigners who chopped wood and carried water. Nobody is left out. This covenant belongs to everyone.

Then Moses takes them back through the story one more time. He reminds them of what they saw in Egypt: the signs, the wonders, the plagues that shattered the most powerful empire on earth. He reminds them of the desert: forty years of wandering, clothes that never wore out, sandals that never fell apart, bread from heaven every morning. He reminds them of the victories over Sihon and Og, the first tangible proof that God was fighting for them.

But then he says something startling: "But to this day the Lord has not given you a mind that understands or eyes that see or ears that hear."

Wait. They've seen all these things and they still don't *see*? They've heard Moses preach for an entire book and they still don't *hear*? What does that mean?

It means there's a difference between witnessing something and understanding it. Their parents watched the Red Sea split apart and still built a golden calf forty days later. You can see a miracle with your eyes and miss its meaning with your heart. Moses is saying that *today*, through these speeches, through this covenant renewal, God is finally opening their understanding. Today is the day they can truly see what it all means.

And what it means is this: everything in their lives, from the plagues in Egypt to the manna in the desert to the victories over the Amorite kings, was God keeping his promise. Every step of the journey was grace. Now it's time to respond.

STANDING BEFORE GOD

The covenant renewal ceremony Moses describes is breathtaking in its scope.

Everyone stands before the Lord: leaders and laborers, men and women, children and foreigners. Moses makes it clear that this covenant is not just for the people standing there that day. It's also for "those who are not here today," meaning every future generation that would come after them. The commitments being made on the plains of Moab reach forward through time. Every generation of God's people would be bound by this covenant, just as every generation would be invited into its blessings.

The purpose of the ceremony is twofold. First, the people are entering into God's sworn covenant, accepting its privileges and its consequences. Second, through this ritual God is confirming them as his people and himself as their God. This is the covenant formula that runs like a golden thread through the entire Bible: "I will be your God, and you will be my people." That promise started with Abraham, was formalized at Sinai, and is being renewed right here on the edge of the Jordan.

Then Moses issues a warning. He knows human nature. He knows that somewhere in the crowd, maybe now, maybe in the future, someone is listening to these curses and secretly thinking, "That won't happen to me. I can follow other gods on the side and still be fine. I'll be safe even if I go my own way."

Moses calls this person out. He says that kind of thinking is like a poisonous root that spreads through the whole community. One person's secret rebellion doesn't stay secret for long. It grows. It infects others. And eventually, the consequences fall not just on the individual but on the entire nation and even on the land itself.

He paints a picture of what the land will look like if Israel breaks the covenant: salt, sulfur, scorched earth, nothing growing, nothing planted, nothing living. Like the destruction of Sodom and Gomorrah. And when foreigners pass through and see the devastation, they'll ask, "Why has the Lord done this to this land?" The answer will be obvious: "Because this people abandoned the covenant of the Lord, the God of their ancestors."

The chapter closes with one of the most mysterious verses in the Bible: "The secret things belong to the Lord our God, but the things revealed belong to us and to our children forever, that we may follow all the words of this law."

Moses is drawing a line. There are things about God's plan

that are beyond human understanding, hidden mysteries that only God knows. But the law, the covenant, the choice between life and death? Those things have been revealed. They're clear. They're knowable. And they're our responsibility. We don't need to unlock cosmic secrets to live faithfully. We just need to obey what God has already made plain.

AFTER THE WORST HAS HAPPENED

If chapter 29 ends in darkness, chapter 30 opens a window of light. Moses looks past the covenant ceremony, past the conquest of the land, past the blessings and the curses, past even the exile he knows is coming, and he sees something on the other side. Restoration.

"When all these blessings and curses I have set before you come on you and you take them to heart wherever the Lord your God disperses you among the nations, and when you and your children return to the Lord your God and obey him with all your heart and with all your soul according to everything I command you today, then the Lord your God will restore your fortunes and have compassion on you and gather you again from all the nations where he scattered you."

Even after the worst-case scenario. Even after exile. Even after the land lies in ruins and the people are scattered to the ends of the earth. If they turn back to God with their whole hearts, he will come for them.

And then Moses makes a promise that reaches into the deepest place: "The Lord your God will circumcise your hearts and the hearts of your descendants, so that you may love him with all your heart and with all your soul, and live."

This is the answer to the problem that has haunted the entire book. Moses has been commanding the people to love God with all their hearts since chapter 6. But he knows, and God knows, that they can't do it on their own. Their hearts are stubborn. Their necks are stiff. The golden calf proved it. The rebellion at Kadesh Barnea proved it. Their entire history proved it.

So God makes a promise: *I will do the surgery myself.* I will remove whatever is blocking you from loving me fully. I will change you from the inside out. This isn't something Israel can achieve by trying harder. It's something God will do for them, as an act of grace.

The prophets later picked up this thread and ran with it. Jeremiah promised a "new covenant" in which God would write his law on people's hearts (Jeremiah 31:33). Ezekiel promised that God would give his people a new heart and put his Spirit within them (Ezekiel 36:26–27). And when Jesus came, he announced that the time had finally arrived. The new covenant, sealed in his blood, would accomplish what the old covenant could only point toward: hearts truly transformed by God's own hand.

NOT TOO HARD, NOT TOO FAR

Then Moses says something that cuts through every excuse anyone has ever made for not following God. "Now what I am commanding you today is not too difficult for you or beyond your reach. It is not up in heaven, so that you have to ask, 'Who will ascend into heaven to get it and proclaim it to us so we may obey it?' Nor is it beyond the sea, so that you have to ask, 'Who will cross the sea to get it and proclaim it to us so we may obey it?' No, the word is very near you; it is in your mouth and in your heart so you may obey it."

God's will isn't hidden on a mountaintop or locked behind a riddle. It isn't a treasure buried at the bottom of the ocean that only spiritual experts can retrieve. It's *right here*. In your mouth, ready to be spoken. In your heart, ready to be lived. God has made his will so accessible, so clear, so close, that the only reason not to follow it is the choice not to.

Paul later quoted this very passage in Romans 10 and connected it to the gospel of Jesus Christ. Just as God's word was near to Israel, Christ is near to us. We don't need to ascend to heaven to find him or descend to the grave to raise him. The word of faith is near, in our mouths and in our hearts.

THE FORK IN THE RIVER

And now we arrive at the climax. Not just of this chapter, but of the entire book. "See, I set before you today life and prosperity, death and destruction. … I have set before you life and death, blessings and curses. Now choose life, so that you and your children may live and that you may love the Lord your God, listen to his voice, and hold fast to him. For the Lord is your life."

Moses calls heaven and earth as witnesses. He's done everything he can. He's taught them, warned them, pleaded with them, retold their story, described both futures with unflinching honesty. Now he steps back and says: the choice is yours.

Choose life. Love God. Listen to his voice. Hold fast to him. For he is your life, and the length of your days in the land he swore to give Abraham, Isaac, and Jacob.

That's it. That's the whole message of Deuteronomy in a single sentence. Everything Moses has said for thirty chapters comes down to this: God has given you everything you need. He's rescued you, loved you, taught you, and placed the choice in your hands. Don't take the safe, empty path that leads nowhere. Choose the one that leads to life.

WHAT THIS MEANS FOR US

First, God's grace doesn't run out. Even after Israel's worst failures, even after exile and devastation, God promises restoration to anyone who returns to him with a whole heart. There is no point at which you have drifted so far that God can't bring you back.

Second, the real problem is the human heart, and only God can fix it. Moses knew that laws and commands alone couldn't change people. What Israel needed, and what we need, is a heart surgery that only God can perform. That's what the new covenant in Jesus provides: not just rules on a page but the Spirit of God living inside us, making us able to love him the way we were designed to.

Third, God's will is not hidden or impossible. It's near. It's clear. It's accessible. The command to love God and follow his ways isn't reserved for spiritual giants. It's for everyone, including you.

Fourth, the choice is real and it's yours. Moses can preach. God can promise. But nobody can choose for you. Every day you face the same two paths: love God or drift away, trust him or go your own way, life or death. And every day, Moses' voice echoes across the centuries: choose life.

TALKING POINTS

1. **Moses said God had not given Israel "eyes that see or ears that hear" until that very day.** What's the difference between witnessing something and truly understanding it? Has there been a moment when something about God suddenly clicked for you?

2. **God promised to "circumcise your hearts," meaning he would do internally what the people couldn't do for themselves.** Why is it important that heart transformation is God's work and not just human effort?

3. **Moses said God's command is "not too difficult" and "not beyond your reach."** Do you ever feel like following God is too hard? How does this verse challenge that feeling?

4. **"Choose life" is one of the most famous commands in the Bible.** What does choosing life look like practically for someone your age, in your daily decisions?

5. **Moses called heaven and earth as witnesses to Israel's choice.** Why do you think he did that? What does it tell us about how seriously God takes our decisions?

Moses has said everything he can say. He's preached his heart out, laid every card on the table, and placed the choice squarely in the people's hands. But his work isn't quite finished. There's still one more thing to do: hand the mantle to Joshua, write down the law, teach the people a song they'll never forget, bless the twelve tribes, and climb a mountain to see the land he'll never enter.

Turn the page.

8

THE DEATH OF MOSES

Homer's *Iliad*, one of the oldest stories ever written, is about the final days of the Trojan War. For ten years, the Greek army has been camped outside the walls of Troy, trying to conquer a city that won't fall. The greatest warrior in the Greek army is Achilles, and he knows something terrible: he will not survive this war. His mother told him long ago that he had a choice. He could go home, live a long and quiet life, and be forgotten. Or he could stay, fight with everything he had, and die young but be remembered forever.

Achilles stays. He fights. He loses his closest friend. He rages. He grieves. And in the end, he gives everything he has to a cause he will never see completed. The *Iliad* doesn't end with the fall of Troy. It ends with a funeral. The war isn't over. The city still stands. But Achilles' story is finished, and the reader knows that what comes next will happen because of what he gave.

There's a reason I'm thinking about Achilles as we open these final chapters of Deuteronomy. Moses, too, has given everything for a mission he will not see completed. He has led this people for forty years through a wilderness that should have killed them all. He has stood between God and Israel more times than he can count, pleading for their lives when God's anger burned. He has preached his heart out on the plains of Moab, pouring the last of his energy into speeches he hopes they'll remember when he's gone.

And now, at the edge of everything he's worked for, with the Promised Land shimmering on the horizon, Moses must stop walking. He will not cross the Jordan. He will not eat the fruit of Canaan. He will not see the walls of Jericho fall.

His story ends here. But the story of God's people is just beginning.

PASSING THE MANTLE

Chapter 31 opens with Moses doing what he's done for forty years: talking to his people. But this time, the tone is different. This isn't a sermon. It's a goodbye.

"I am now a hundred and twenty years old," he tells them, "and I am no longer able to lead you. The Lord has said to me, 'You shall not cross the Jordan.'"

Those words must have landed like a stone in the people's stomachs. Moses had been their leader, their pastor, their connection to God for as long as any of them could remember. For most of this generation, there had never been a day without Moses. And now he was telling them he wouldn't be coming with them.

But Moses doesn't let them sink into despair. In the very next breath, he redirects their eyes: "The Lord your God himself will cross over ahead of you. He will destroy these nations before you, and you will take possession of their land. Joshua also will cross over ahead of you, as the Lord said."

Notice the order. God first, Joshua second. Moses wants them to understand that their future doesn't depend on any human leader, not even him. It depends on God. Joshua will be a capable commander, but the one who actually wins battles, keeps promises, and never abandons his people is the Lord himself.

Then Moses turns to Joshua and speaks directly to him, in front of the entire nation: "Be strong and courageous. Do not be afraid or terrified because of them, for the Lord your God goes with you; he will never leave you nor forsake you."

Be strong. Be courageous. God is with you. He won't let go. Those words would follow Joshua for the rest of his life. God himself would repeat them almost word for word after Moses died (Joshua 1:5–9). They became the foundation on which Joshua built an entire campaign of conquest.

THE TORAH AND THE SONG

Moses does two remarkable things before he dies. Both are about ensuring that his voice will outlast his life.

First, he writes down the entire Torah, the collection of teachings and laws he has been proclaiming, and hands it to the Levitical priests and the elders of Israel. He instructs them to read it aloud to the entire nation every seven years at the Festival of Booths. Men, women, children, and foreigners, everyone is to gather and hear the words of the covenant. Moses knows that memory fades. Commitment erodes. The generation standing before him may be passionate today, but their grandchildren won't remember this moment unless someone reads these words to them.

The written Torah is Moses' gift to every future generation. He can't be there in person, but his words can. Every time the Torah is read aloud, Moses' voice echoes across the centuries, calling God's people back to faithfulness.

Second, God tells Moses to teach the people a song. Not another speech. A *song*. God knows something about human nature: people forget sermons, but they remember songs. The lyrics get stuck in your head. The melody comes back to you when you're walking down the road, lying in bed at night, working in the field. A song can go everywhere a person goes, even when a leader can't.

The Song of Moses in chapter 32 is like a national anthem for Israel. It covers everything: the perfection of God, the history of his grace toward Israel, the tragedy of Israel's inevitable unfaithfulness, the judgment that would follow, and the hope that in the end, God's compassion would triumph over his anger. It's beautiful and devastating at the same time. In one long poem, Moses compressed everything he'd been preaching into lyrics the people could carry with them forever.

The song opens with an image that captures its purpose: "Let my teaching fall like rain and my words descend like dew." Moses' final words are meant to soak into the soil of their hearts and make something grow.

A BLESSING FOR EVERY TRIBE

Chapter 33 records Moses' final act of pastoral care: a blessing spoken over each of the twelve tribes. Like a father gathering his children one last time, Moses pronounces words of hope, identity, and purpose over every family in the nation.

The blessings vary. Some are long, some are short. Some are clear, others are poetic and mysterious. But together they paint a picture of a people who are deeply loved by God and destined for something great. Moses opens with a stunning description of God arriving in blazing glory from Sinai, "with myriads of holy ones" and "a flaming fire at his right hand." He closes with a declaration that has echoed through the ages: "There is no one like the God of Jeshurun, who rides across the heavens to help you and on the clouds in his majesty. The eternal God is your refuge, and underneath are the everlasting arms."

Underneath are the everlasting arms. Whatever happens next, whatever failures and victories and heartbreaks lie ahead for these twelve tribes, they will never fall out of God's hands. The arms underneath them are everlasting. That's the last theological truth Moses speaks over his people: you are held.

THE MOUNTAIN

Then comes chapter 34, and the pace slows to something almost unbearable.

Moses climbs Mount Nebo, alone. He walks up from the plains of Moab, step by step, leaving behind the camp, the people, the tabernacle, everything he's known for forty years. He climbs to the summit of Pisgah, and from there, God shows him everything.

He sees it all. The entire Promised Land, spread out before him like a painting. Gilead to the north. The territory of Judah to the south. The western sea. The Negev desert. The palm trees of Jericho. Every inch of the land God swore to Abraham, to Isaac, and to Jacob.

"I have let you see it with your eyes," God tells him, "but you will not cross over into it."

And then Moses dies.

The text doesn't dramatize it. There are no final words recorded. No deathbed speech. Just this: "Moses the servant of the Lord died there in Moab, as the Lord had said." The greatest prophet Israel ever knew took his last breath on a mountaintop, with the Promised Land filling his eyes, and God standing beside him.

What happens next is one of the most extraordinary details in the entire Bible: "He buried him in Moab, in the valley opposite Beth Peor, but to this day no one knows where his grave is."

God himself buried Moses. No human hands. No marked tomb. No monument. No pilgrimages. Just God, laying to rest the man who had served him for a hundred and twenty years, in a grave that would never be found.

Why hide the grave? Perhaps because God knew his people. If they could visit Moses' tomb, they might worship it. They might make it a shrine. They might elevate the servant to the place that belongs only to the Master. By concealing the grave, God ensured that Israel's attention would remain where Moses himself had always pointed it: toward God alone.

NO ONE LIKE HIM

The book closes with a tribute that feels like it was written with tears. "Since then, no prophet has risen in Israel like Moses, whom the Lord knew face to face, who did all those signs and wonders the Lord sent him to do in Egypt, to Pharaoh and to all his officials and to his whole land. For no one has ever shown the mighty power or performed the awesome deeds that Moses did in the sight of all Israel."

No one like him. Not since. That's how the narrator measures the gap Moses left behind. No one with his access to God. No one with his courage before Pharaoh. No one with his power, his faithfulness, his stubborn, heartbroken love for a people who never quite deserved it.

Moses was not perfect. He argued with God at the burning bush. He struck the rock when God told him to speak to it. He blamed the people for his own punishment. He was human in every sense of the word.

But he was faithful. For forty years, through rebellion and plague and war and thirst, he kept leading. He kept teaching. He kept praying. He kept pointing people to God when they wanted to go anywhere else. And when it was time to go, he didn't cling to power. He handed the mantle to Joshua, wrote down the Torah, taught the people a song, blessed the tribes, and climbed the mountain.

He went to God the same way he had lived for God: obediently, with his eyes on the promise.

WHAT THIS MEANS FOR US

First, faithfulness matters more than finishing. Moses never entered the Promised Land. By most measures, his mission was incomplete. But God never called him a failure. He called him "my servant." Faithfulness isn't about crossing the finish line yourself. It's about running your leg of the race and handing off the baton well. Moses did that better than anyone.

Second, God's work outlasts every human leader. Moses was irreplaceable, and yet God's plan continued without him. Joshua took over. The Jordan was crossed. The land was conquered. The story didn't stop because one man died, even the greatest man who ever lived. God's purposes don't depend on any single person. They depend on God.

Third, what you leave behind matters more than what you accomplish. Moses' greatest legacy wasn't a military victory or a political achievement. It was a written Torah, a song, and a generation of people who had heard the voice of God through him. The things that outlast us are the words we speak into other people's lives and the faith we pass on.

Fourth, the story points to someone greater. The narrator says no prophet like Moses ever arose in Israel. But centuries later, on another mountain, Jesus stood with Moses and Elijah, and a voice from heaven said, "This is my Son, whom I love. Listen to him" (Mark 9:7). Moses mediated God's word to Israel. Jesus *is* the Word of God. Moses brought the people to the edge of the Promised Land. Jesus brings us all the way home. Everything Moses pointed toward, Jesus fulfilled.

TALKING POINTS

1. **Moses told Israel, "The Lord your God goes with you; he will never leave you nor forsake you."** How does it change your perspective to know that God's faithfulness doesn't depend on human leaders?

2. **God told Moses to teach the people a song, not just another speech.** Why do you think music has such power

to shape what we believe and remember? What songs have shaped your faith?

3. **Moses blessed each tribe before he died, speaking words of identity and hope over them.** Has anyone ever spoken words over you that stuck with you and shaped how you see yourself?

4. **God buried Moses in a hidden grave so no one could turn it into a shrine.** What does this tell you about God's priorities? Why is it important that we worship God and not his servants?

5. **The narrator says no prophet like Moses ever arose in Israel.** How does Jesus fulfill and surpass what Moses started? In what ways is Jesus "greater than Moses"?

The book of Deuteronomy ends on a mountaintop with an empty horizon. Moses is gone. The Jordan still has to be crossed. The battles still have to be fought. The land still has to be claimed. Nothing is finished yet.

But everything is in place. The Torah has been written. The song has been taught. The successor has been commissioned. The blessings have been spoken. The choice between life and death has been laid out in terms no one can misunderstand.

And underneath it all, holding every promise together, are the everlasting arms of a God who never forgets, never fails, and never lets go.

The story of Moses is over. But the story of God and his people stretches forward, through Joshua and the judges, through kings and prophets, through exile and return, through four hundred years of silence, and finally to a night in Bethlehem when another baby was born who would lead his people out of a deeper bondage and into a better land.

Moses pointed to that day. He never saw it. But he believed it was coming.

And it did.